ELEPHANTS IN SHELLS

Everyone believes that he or she can recognize a tortoise, but actually the word is misused as often as it is correctly applied. This book is about only one definition of a tortoise: a highly terrestrial turtle that lacks webbing between the toes of any of the feet and is a member of the family Testudinidae. Tortoises do *not* include box turtles (genus *Terrapene*) of the family Emydidae (the water turtles), and of course they do not include the various snake-necked aquatic species that the Aussies like to call water tortoises. Here we are going to discuss some of the more available tortoises, about 20 or so species of the 40 species recognized in the more recent checklists of the family. We'll also mention a few other species and genera in passing because of their interest to the more advanced hobbyist and the possibility that they will show up in the local pet shop in the future.

WHAT ARE TORTOISES?

Yes, I realize that about half my books carry a similar subhead or chapter head, but it is important that we know just what turtles we are discussing before we proceed. Tortoises are very special turtles with a long fossil record over much of the world (except Australia and the neighboring islands of the southern Pacific). They have been present since at least the Eocene (50 or so million years ago) and are very well adapted for what most of them do. With few exceptions, they are vegetarians in nature, feeding on a variety of fruits, leaves, and even dry grasses. Only a few species are found near water, and even fewer regularly take significant amounts of meat in their diets. They are the grazers of the reptile world, equivalent to antelopes, bison, and even elephants in some respects, and showing among themselves almost as much diversity.

The typical tortoise has a

PHOTO BY P. FREED

A "typical" tortoise, the Travancore Tortoise, *Geochelone forsteni*, showing the usual features of the group: elephant-like limbs, dull coloration, and domed shell.

somewhat domed or convex upper shell (carapace), front legs that end in heavy claws and are flattened so the knees almost touch when the animal withdraws into the shell, and tree-like hind legs that end in oval feet with heavy cushioning at the bottom and short, heavy claws. Most tortoises have brown legs and heads, often with spots or blotches of red or yellow; they never have bright stripes on the legs like many water turtles. Males of most tortoises have long, thick tails and deeply concave hind plastra (the lower shell) that allow them to stand almost erect at the back of the female's shell during mating. Male turtles often are quite vocal during mating, giving voice to assorted grunts, groans, pips, and even higher pitched screams.

Tortoises share with other turtles basic divisions of the horny plates (scutes) covering the bony shell. Basically, the carapace (top shell, remember?) when seen from above is encircled by many smaller scutes known as *marginals*, while down the center of the carapace is a single row of large, squarish *vertebrals* (also known as centrals). On each side of the vertebral row and between the marginals is a row of large *costals* (often but less familiarly called pleurals). Thus the marginals are paired scutes and so are the costals, while the vertebrals are singles. In some tortoises there is an unpaired *cervical* (also called nuchal) scute between the anteriormost marginals and directly over the center of the neck. The most posterior marginals on each side (over the tail) are the supracaudals, important scutes when they are fused into a single scute in a few species. The scutes of the lower shell (plastron) and the arch that connects the upper and lower shells (the bridge) also have special names, but I won't bother you with them here because they seldom will be important in our discussions.

Identifying the common tortoises seldom presents a problem. If you see webs between the toes of the hind feet, you don't have a tortoise but instead have a box turtle or some other water turtle adapted to live mostly on land. The common tortoise species are easily told apart by size and color patterns, plus a few more technical characters of the scutes. Unlike many herps, you can just pick up a tortoise and check out its scutes with the naked eye to make fairly positive identifications.

HOW MANY TORTOISES?

As in most groups of animals, there is disagreement among experts as to exactly how many tortoises there are and just what to call them and how to group them. For your convenience, and because several of the species will not be mentioned elsewhere in this book, the following is a list of what seem to be the most typically recognized genera and species of tortoises.

Chersina angulata, Bowsprit Tortoise

Geochelone carbonaria, Red-footed Tortoise

Geochelone chilensis, Chaco Tortoise

Geochelone denticulata Yellow-footed Tortoise

Geochelone elegans, Indian Star Tortoise

Geochelone elongata, Elongated Tortoise

Geochelone forsteni, Travancore Tortoise

Geochelone gigantea, Aldabra Giant Tortoise

Geochelone nigra, Galapagos Giant Tortoise

Geochelone pardalis, Leopard Tortoise

Geochelone platynota, Burmese Star Tortoise

Geochelone radiata, Radiated Tortoise

Geochelone sulcata, African Spurred Tortoise

Geochelone yniphora, Angulated Tortoise

Gopherus agassizi, Desert Tortoise

Gopherus berlandieri, Texas Tortoise

Gopherus flavomarginatus, Bolson Tortoise

Gopherus polyphemus, Gopher Tortoise

Homopus areolatus, Parrot-beaked Cape Tortoise

Homopus bergeri, Berger's Cape Tortoise

Homopus boulengeri, Boulenger's Cape Tortoise

Homopus femoralis, Karroo Cape Tortoise

Homopus signatus, Speckled Cape Tortoise

Kinixys belliana, Bell's Hinge-back Tortoise

Kinixys erosa, Forest Hinge-back Tortoise

Kinixys homeana, Home's Hinge-back Tortoise

Kinixys natalensis, Natal Hinge-back Tortoise

Malacochersus tornieri, Pancake Tortoise

Manouria emys, Mountain Tortoise

Manouria impressa, Impressed Tortoise

Psammobates geometricus, Geometric Tortoise

Psammobates oculiferus, Serrated Star Tortoise

Psammobates tentorius, Tent Tortoise

Pyxis arachnoides, Spider

PHOTO BY P. A. RUTLEDGE

Recent successes in captive-breeding some tortoises have led to an availability of some species, such as these little African Spurs, *Geochelone sulcata,* that formerly seldom were seen in private hands.

Tortoise

Pyxis planicauda, Flat-shelled Tortoise

Testudo graeca, Spur-thighed Tortoise

Testudo hermanni, Hermann's Tortoise

Testudo horsfieldi, Central Asian Tortoise

Testudo kleinmanni, Egyptian Tortoise

Testudo marginata, Marginated Tortoise

Many of these species have subspecies, and in several cases some experts feel that more full species should be recognized. Additionally, several of these genera have been broken up into smaller units. This is especially so in the genus *Geochelone*, where a genus *Indotestudo* often is recognized for the Elongated and Travancore Tortoises and other genera are distinguished by some. Since this is not a book on tortoise identification, I'll stick to the generally more familiar names.

GENERAL TORTOISE CARE

Because tortoises are so diverse in their requirements, we'll have to cover their requirements as we discuss the species. In general, however, tortoises are vegetarians that eat a variety of fruits and greens and vegetables (the veggie salad), like it warm all year, and cannot tolerate drafts. Species from deserts and dry plains, such as the Central Asian, Gopher, and Geometric Tortoises, among many others, cannot tolerate high humidity. This means that if you live in a humid climate, you will have little luck with such species unless you can afford to give them humidity-controlled quarters. In such cases you might want to consider a species that is more adapted to wetter savannahs or forest edges.

In many respects the best pet tortoises are the larger species such as the Red-footed, African Spurred, and Leopard. Though they often are expensive to purchase, they grow fast, are very tolerant of climate (as long as extremes are avoided), and because of their large body volume stay at more uniform temperatures than smaller species and thus are less subject to respiratory infections (at least once they've grown a bit). Large tortoises eat like pigs, while smaller tortoises may be difficult to start feeding. Large tortoises also need heated outdoor housing much of the year.

Selection

If at all possible, try to purchase a captive-bred tortoise. Several species are being bred in fair numbers and are readily available through your local pet shop, though perhaps your dealer may have to put in a special order for you. Many tortoises around the world are threatened by loss of habitat through human-caused changes in the forests and plains or simply through being collected for the food, souvenir, and pet markets. Wild-caught tortoises often are scarred, have dangerous infestations of intestinal worms, and may be adapted to very narrow climatic and food requirements you will never be able to match in the home. Never buy a tortoise that is totally inactive, feels "hollow" when picked up, has runny or puffy eyes, or is blowing bubbles through the nose. In fact, if any tortoise in an establishment has a runny, wet nose, the odds are great that all the tortoises in the shop may be infected with a dangerous respiratory disease. Always quarantine new tortoise additions for at least six weeks, making sure that nothing you or they touch is shared with any other tortoises (or turtles) in your home. Because most tortoises are expensive, long-lived creatures, it is a good idea to have a veterinarian on call and to have your new purchase examined immediately after it leaves the shop. There no longer is any reason for a pet tortoise to die in your home after only one or two years in captivity.

Quarters

With few exceptions, tortoises need to be able to spend most of the day outdoors during the warm season. Smaller individuals and species can be kept in large terraria, but they may never grow well and always will seem a bit weak and out of color. In most areas of the Northern Hemisphere, tortoises will have to be brought indoors during cool months and even on cool, damp spring and autumn evenings. Most hobbyists, however, probably will at least start with a small tortoise that can be kept parttime in a terrarium.

The terrarium should be as large as possible. Many hobbyists let their tortoises run free in the house if there are no other pets, making sure there are no dangers such as openings in the walls, doors to get stuck in, or insecticides and rodent poisons exposed; tortoises are very strong and can wedge their way through very narrow crevices behind appliances and partially open doors. If you are using a glass or plastic cage, make sure it is covered to keep out cats and children (as well as casual visitors who may literally want to take your pet home with them).

PHOTO BY P. A. RUTLEDGE

A well-built (almost fancy) tortoise shed for the gigantic African Spurred Tortoise, *Geochelone sulcata*. A shed has to be built to withstand large, strong, determined animals.

An exceptional Red-footed Tortoise, *Geochelone carbonaria*. The amount of red on the head of these animals varies greatly. Captive-breds make hardy, long-lived pets in the proper surroundings. Photo: A. Norman.

Newspaper is the best bedding material because it is cheap, absorbent, and not likely to be eaten by the turtle. Most other substrate materials can be dangerous if eaten, causing bowel impactions. Alfalfa pellets often are recommended, while ground corn cob often is mentioned as dangerous.

Full-spectrum fluorescent lights are required for all species. Buy the best brand your shop has to offer, replace them often, and keep them clean. Light periods of about 10 to 12 hours per day should be sufficient. A good basking light also should be stationed at one end of the terrarium to help make sure the tortoise can rapidly raise its core temperature to functional levels that allow it to feed and move about comfortably.

Most tortoises need a daytime air and substrate temperature of about 80 to 85°F (27 to 30°C), dropping by five to ten degrees at night. This temperature should be maintained all year for most tortoises and certainly for the young of almost all species. Your basking light will help maintain suitable temperatures, but you probably also will need an undertank heating pad of some type at night.

Tortoises need water both to drink and in which to soak. Even desert species drink large amounts of clean, preferably dechlorinated water. Since the same container probably will be used both for drinking and soaking, the water must be changed each day and whenever you notice it is dirty. Some tortoises can produce very large amounts of waste when they soak.

PHOTO COURTESY OF TETRA TERRAFAUNA

High quality prepared foods only recently have been made specifically for tortoises. They are convenient and offer a well-balanced diet when supplemented by fruits and vegetables.

Juveniles

Baby tortoises grow slowly, and most species take at least one or two years before they begin to resemble adults in hardiness. Until then they must be treated with kid gloves and never allowed to become too cool, too hot, too wet, or too dry. Each group of tortoises has its own requirements, so be sure to get exacting instructions if you purchase a baby tortoise. As a general rule, babies need a bit warmer temperatures and more exposure to balanced sunlight than adults. Some tortoises (especially those of the genus *Testudo*) need to be kept at cooler temperatures during the winter; young turtles often do not survive avocado, tomatoes) fed every other day. The choice of foods of course can be changed to reflect seasonal availability and your budget. Just make sure that everything is clean (no pesticides, herbicides, insecticides, heavy fertilizers) and fresh (you'd never eat rotten apples, so why should your pet?). Many adult tortoises will eat small

PHOTO BY P. A. RUTLEDGE

A small male African Spur checking out a female. With proper care, a hatchling Spur may mature in four to seven years.

this winter cooling (brumation), one of the factors that makes these genera very difficult to keep and breed successfully.

Feeding

Most tortoises do well of a mixture of chopped greens (spinach, green lettuce, kale, collards, dandelion), vegetables (carrots, green beans, pumpkin, squash), flowers (dandelion), and fruits (apples, prickly pear, amounts of dog food and moistened monkey chow without harm; the high protein levels in these foods may be dangerous for subadult tortoises, however, causing growth that is too fast and distorts the shell while shortening the lifetime. Leopard Tortoises and the hinge-back tortoises seem to tolerate dog food well compared to the species of *Testudo*, for instance.

The Great Outdoors

If at all possible, your tortoises should spend several hours in the sun each day that the weather is not too humid or breezy. Provide a sturdy pen of wire mesh (the size is not that important) set up so the tortoise can graze on grass and veggie salad in the sun but can retreat to shade when it home at night and not left outdoors from late afternoon to early morning.

If larger tortoises (such as the Leopard and African Spurred) are kept, you probably will find that they prefer a shed to retreat to each evening. You'll need to build an insulated structure at leat 3 feet by 5 feet at the base and high

PHOTO BY K. H. SWITAK

Some tortoises are protected by international and national laws and require special permits if they are to be kept in captivity. One such is the Radiated Tortoise, *Geochelone radiata* of Madagascar.

desires; direct sun will quickly kill even desert tortoises. Make sure there is water present. Baby tortoises have a tendency to eat rocks, bits of glass, seeds, and other debris that may cause intestinal problems, so some keepers make sure the tortoises only sun over carefully raked sand areas. In most areas, all tortoises must be returned to the enough for you to go in to clean it regularly. There should be basking lights at one end and perhaps heating pads at the other, with a bowl of water for soaking. Tortoises soon learn to use a ramp to go to bed at night in their shed. There should be doors that can be closed at night to prevent drafts.

GENERAL GUIDE TO BREEDING TORTOISES

Breeding

Most tortoises mate in much the same way. A male (usually recognizable by its larger size, long and thick tail, and concave determine that it is another male. If not, he moves to the back of the tortoise and sniffs the cloaca to confirm the new turtle as a female. At that point the female attempts to run away, but the male bites her hind legs and rams her shell to make her stop and

A Hermann's Tortoise, *Testudo hermanni*, heading for its shed. Many tortoises kept outdoors part of the year grow better and have a better chance of reproducing than those housed indoors all the time.

or dished out posterior plastron) accidentally stumbles onto a female or her scent trail. If ready to breed (remember, tortoises mature slowly, often not before an age of four or five years, often much more), he faces the female and begins to determine her sex. Often tortoises have complicated head-waving behaviors that are signals of their sex; if the other tortoise responds with certain head waves, the male can submit. He maneuvers into a partially upright position behind her, swings his tail under hers so the cloacas match, and uses his front legs on her shell to balance himself. Usually mating is fairly prolonged and noisy in tortoises, males being quite vocal.

A month or a year later (very variable with species and individuals), the female prepares to lay her rounded eggs by digging a flask-shaped nest in suitable soil. The eggs are laid rapidly, occasionally cracking as they hit one another after a long drop from the female's cloaca, and then the female fills in the hole. Nesting females often are quite shy, so discretion while observing may be necessary. Most keepers remove the eggs to an incubator immediately.

Incubation

Tortoise eggs are incubated much like other reptile eggs. The eggs are placed on a layer of damp vermiculite in a sealable container and then covered with damp vermiculite until just a bit of the egg (for respiration) is left uncovered. The container is removed to a uniformly heated brooder or floated in a heated aquarium and left at the proper temperature (with little variation)

Many different types of bedding or substrate materials are available. Choose a bedding that is safe if ingested, will not mildew, and is biodegradable.

for about 90 to 150 days.

As a general rule, tortoises that come from moist habitats (Redfoots, Mountain Tortoises, etc.) need damper vermiculite (about equal parts water and vermiculite) kept at somewhat lower temperatures (average 80°F,

To lay her clutch, a female tortoise must have access to soil of the proper texture and humidity. The breeder probably will remove the eggs of this Elongated Tortoise, *Geochelone elongata*, as soon as the female finishes laying.

A mating pair of large African Spurred Tortoises, *Geochelone sulcata*. Notice the strongly recurved anterior marginals (the curved scutes at the anterior edge of the shell) of the male, a character typical of the species and the origin of the scientific name.

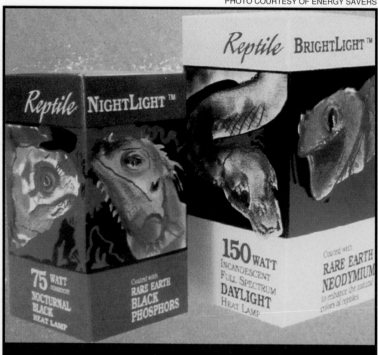

Most tortoises are creatures of the sun, and they need strong basking lights to thrive. Be sure to use a bulb that is designed for reptiles, not an ordinary household lamp.

26.5°C) than desert and dry plains species, which tolerate a mix of one part of water to two parts of vermiculite and an average temperature of about 83°F (28.5°C). Sex in tortoises is determined by the temperature under which the eggs develop, with lower temperatures yielding males. A variation of about 2° F in each direction should lead to increased chances of offspring of both sexes.

Oh yes, be sure to mark the top of the egg as soon as you remove it from the nest pit. After a few hours, the embryo attaches to the shell and cannot be rotated without facing the risk of suffocating or drowning under the weight of its own wastes. Most keeper are emphatic that turtle eggs should never be rotated—always keep the same side up.

Few beginners, and not that many more professionals, have much luck breeding and raising their tortoises, but the number increases each year. Many tortoises have never been bred in captivity and others have never yielded commercial numbers of young. Established, healthy, captive-bred adults are your best bet for successfully reproducing any species.

PHOTO BY **R. D. BARTLETT**

The eggs of most tortoises are round, often ping-pong ball shaped, and white. If laid in rapid succession, it is not uncommon for one or more eggs to crack. Sometimes these recover, so give them a chance after you carefully move them to an incubator.

PHOTO BY P. FREED

Hatching of a Bowsprit Tortoise, *Chersina angulata*. The sculptured pattern at the center of each scute of a hatchling is caused by the textured internal surface of the egg shell pressing against the growing scute of the embryo.

PHOTO BY R. D. BARTLETT

While in the egg, the baby tortoise is literally folded across the middle of its shell. At hatching the shell begins to unfold and exerts pressure against the egg shell, allowing the eggtooth to slice through the egg so the baby can begin to breathe air. Photo of *Geochelone elongata*.

THE MEDITERRANEAN CROWD

THE GENUS *TESTUDO*

When you mention the word tortoise to European herp keepers, they will immediately think of a member of this genus. For decades it was traditional to keep a *Testudo* in the backyard garden or conservatory in England and parts of Europe, a practice that has only recently been ended by laws restricting or prohibiting import of tortoises from southern Europe and northern Africa. Two of the species, Hermann's Tortoise (*T. hermanni*) and the Spur-thighed or Greek Tortoise (*T. graeca*), have been covered in detail by Brian Pursall in his book *Mediterranean Tortoises* (T.F.H. Publications, RE-135). Anyone planning on keeping one of these tortoises **must** read this book to discover how to keep it alive and healthy. Suffice it to say that they are species with very special needs as regards temperature and calcium requirements and are not for the beginner.

The five species of *Testudo* often are confused by hobbyists. The Egyptian Tortoise, *T. kleinmanni*, is a small species (under 6 inches, 15 cm) with five claws on the front foot (as in most other tortoises). Its carapace is high-domed but drops abruptly at the back. Colors are simple, bright sandy tan with narrow dark brown edges to the scutes. The Central Asian Tortoise, *T.*

horsfieldi, is a virtually round tortoise with a low carapace that is mostly dark brown with narrow tan edges to the scutes. Unlike other tortoises (except one subspecies of hinge-back), it has only four claws on the front foot. These two species often are seen in captivity, though recently the Egyptian Tortoise (sometimes called Kleinmann's Tortoise to confuse the authorities) has been placed in Appendix I of the CITES listing, making it essentially an

If you plan on keeping a Mediterranean tortoise, you should have a copy of Brian Pursall's book on the subject (T.F.H. RE-135).

endangered species and virtually impossible to import.

The Marginated Tortoise (*T. marginata*) is large (to 12 inches, 30 cm) and has a distinctly elongated shape with nearly parallel sides. The rear edge of the plastron is strongly flared, the corners of some of the marginals project like weak sawteeth, and there is only one supracaudal scale. Its color is variable, but usually it is dark brown to blackish above with small yellowish tan blotches on each carapace scute; the plastron is yellow with large, paired triangular black blotches.

Most often confused are the Spur-thighed Tortoise (*T. graeca*) and Hermann's Tortoise (*T. hermanni*), which formed the vast majority of tortoises kept in Europe. Both are more or less oval in shape with domed carapaces that are sandy tan with large, irregular angled dark brown triangles or blotches. In Hermann's Tortoise the plastron is yellowish with two wide dark brown bands running from front to back. There are two supracaudal scales, and the male's tail ends in a large claw-like scale. *T. graeca* is quite variable in adult size, shell shape, and coloration, but it can be distinguished easily by structural characters. There is almost always only one supracaudal scute, and the tip of the male's tail ends in normal scales. The best character, however, is the presence of a large, often pointed, tubercle at the back of the thigh that never is developed in Hermann's Tortoise.

THE MEDITERRANEAN TORTOISES'S WORLD

Testudo species are inhabitants of plains, deserts, and woodland edges from southern Europe to Pakistan and Morocco to Israel.

PHOTO BY J. MERLI

A group of baby Spur-thighed or "Greek" Tortoises, *Testudo graeca*. Though attractive and sometimes inexpensive, baby Mediterranean tortoises often fare poorly in captivity.

PHOTO BY R. D. BARTLETT

Baby tortoises, like this Hermann's, *Testudo hermanni*, have the scutes of the carapace (top shell) without growth rings, only the sculptured embryonic scute being present. As they grow, they add rings to the outside of each scute and the embryonic scute becomes proportionately smaller.

They are adapted to cool or cold winters, very hot summers, and long periods between rains. This has made them among the hardest tortoises to maintain in captivity because each species tends to have strange requirements. The Egyptian Tortoise, for instance, is a species of deserts and shrubby desert edges, and it is unable to adapt to humidity higher than 40 or 50%; it is active during the winter in its Libyian to Negev, Israel, range, disappearing into cover during the hot summers. The Central Asian Tortoise ranges from the Caspian Sea to Pakistan, an area including steppes and near-deserts that may be frozen for months on end and broil during the summer. The species burrows during the winter and then again during the summer if the temperature reaches much above 86°F (30°C); it also cannot tolerate high humidity.

Marginated Tortoises are native only to southern Greece and adjacent islands, an area with dry, scrubby, rocky hills. Hermann's Tortoise is truly a species of the Mediterranean, occurring along the northern coast from southern France to Turkey, plus the Balkans and central Mediterranean islands. The most wide-ranging species is stone and must be removed by a veterinarian if the female is to survive. Pursall emphasizes that Mediterranean tortoises are not social animals and they are best kept alone; the sexes must never be mixed.

Young *Testudo* are vegetarians that do not react well to animal protein. They need tremendous amounts of calcium in the diet to grow correctly, and generally can be considered tough tortoises unless you live in a warm, very dry climate.

THE CENTRAL ASIAN TORTOISE

Currently the only Mediterranean tortoise that is commonly seen in captivity is *T. horsfieldi* from the Russian steppes. It is imported in large numbers, usually as adults or half-grown specimens, but seldom lives for more than a year or two. They can be wintered at about 42 to 46°F (5 to 8°C) for up to five months, making sure that the gut is completely empty and also that water is present just in case the tortoises wake up briefly. When they are brought out of brumation in February or March, they

PHOTO BY R. D. BARTLETT

The Central Asian or Russian Steppes Tortoise, *Testudo horsfieldi*, often is available cheaply. The mostly dark shell with narrow pale rings around the scutes is not very attractive to most hobbyists.

PHOTO BY R. D. BARTLETT

This young Marginated Tortoise, *Testudo marginata*, shows the rings of at least four seasons of growth. Not years, seasons—a change from hot to cold, dry to wet, or plenty of food to little food. You cannot accurately age tortoises by the number of scute rings.

should be bathed several times in luke-warm water to help free the kidneys from calcium deposits accumulated during the winter. Provide a hot basking area and undertank heating, but allow the temperature to drop by as much as 10°F during the night (more might be better here if you can afford to experiment). Remember, these tortoises come from a very marginal, difficult habitat that is not exactly a land of milk and honey. The sexes (check for a longer tail in the male and a deep concavity in his plastron) should be kept separately. The tortoises definitely enjoy warm spring days outdoors in a protected shed or greenhouse. They feed on fruits, greens, and flowers like many other tortoises.

The species has been bred in captivity very rarely so far. Mating occurred when a male was put with a female shortly after brumation ended and was very active and violent as in many tortoises, with much biting and shell butting. The mating period lasted about a month, and six weeks later the female laid three eggs in a shallow hole. When incubated at about 50% humidity and 82 to 86°F (28 to 30°C), dropping a bit at night, the eggs hatched in from 73 to 92 days. (Natural incubation times appear to be 90 to 120 days.) The young ate only greens for the first year and would not take fruit or flowers; they ate sand grains immediately after hatching. Growth was slow, the young only doubling their weight during the

SPURS AND SPOTS

The largest tortoises kept by "average" hobbyists are the African Spurred (*Geochelone sulcata*) and Leopard (*Geochelone pardalis*) Tortoises. The Spurred is a true giant among tortoises, the third largest species and the largest non-island form, and the Leopard is no slouch when it comes to size either. These are perhaps the hardiest of the tortoises once they pass childhood, but unfortunately they are too large for many hobbyists. They are not really suitable for apartments and do best if they can have access to outdoor housing most of the year.

Both species come from dry African savannahs, and in the United States they typically do best as pets and breeders when kept in California, Arizona, and states with similar climates. They do not really thrive in cool, humid climates even if given sufficient heating and lighting. Captive-bred Leopard Tortoises, however, are becoming more common and affordable and seem to be more adaptable than specimens of just a generation or two ago.

PHOTO BY P. A. RUTLEDGE

African Spurs are slow to mature. Specimens under 24 to 28 inches in shell length may be almost impossible to sex correctly.

AFRICAN SPURS

The African Spurred Tortoise, *G. sulcata*, is resident in a narrow band across northern Africa just at the southern edge of the Sahara Desert. As you might · expect, they like warm, dry climates and do best if kept at a nearly constant 80 to 86°F (27 to 30°F), with a little drop at night. They commonly exceed 30 inches (75 cm) in length and over 120 pounds (45.5 kilos) in weight. In color Spurs are one of the plainest tortoises, being a nearly uniform light brown over the entire shell and body. One of its distinguishing features is the strongly developed, often curled, anterior and posterior marginals, which may be especially obvious

Above: If fed too much protein (i.e., animal snacks of various types) when young, the carapace of the African Spur may become deformed, the scutes becoming pyramids. Photo by P.A. Rutledge

Below: Mating in *Geochelone sulcata* may be a noisy affair, with much groaning and shell banging. The curved marginals of older males seldom are found in females. Photo by P.A. Rutledge

in large males; another character is the presence of two or three long, pointed, conical spurs on the back of each thigh. Like many other tortoises, the males are significantly larger than the females; they may be difficult to sex until fully mature at a shell length of about 24 inches (60 cm),

A small adult female African Spur and several young. (Note carapace deformities in the young due to improper diet.) It commonly takes seven years for these turtles to mature sexually and 15 or 20 years for them to reach full size.

when males can be told by their longer tails and slightly concave posterior plastrons.

Such a large tortoise presents problems in housing. They may dig burrows over 20 feet (6 meters) long and can go through walls, porches, and housing foundations. They are dangerous to have in an apartment because of the havoc they can cause when just moving around, and must be kept outdoors. Provide them with an insulated house (with doors that can be closed to keep in the heat) at least 3 X 5 feet in floor area, larger, of course, if you plan on keeping a breeding trio of a male and two females. The tortoises will learn to enter their house when the temperature outdoors drops to 65°F (18°C) or so. Use heating pads and basking lights to keep the house at close to a constant 80 to 86°F (27 to 30°C). Feed them the usual veggie salad and expect to have to clean up a lot of mess; big turtles leave horse-sized piles of mess.

Mating proceeds as usual for tortoises, being rather violent and sometimes loud. Females lay round white eggs larger than ping-pong balls, often producing several clutches of a dozen or more eggs each year. The babies are pale yellowish tan with darker scute margins and often a single dark brown spot near the center of each scute. Babies can be kept indoors their first year in a suitably heated and lighted terrarium. Maturity may take four to seven years, and the tortoises could live well over 75 years.

ADAPTABLE LEOPARDS

One of the most widely distributed species of tortoise, the Leopard (*G. pardalis*) is found in savannahs from the Sudan and the Horn of Africa south to the Cape and then north in southwestern Africa   to Angola. Over this area it varies quite a bit in size, shape, and coloration, but usually it is a beautifully marked tortoise of more than average size. Adults are pale tan (sometimes almost whitish), covered on the carapace with black spots and blotches that tend to accumulate along the growth lines of the scutes. Large adults may be nearly plain brown, but this is not common. Like its cousin the African Spurred Tortoise, there are two or three conical spurs behind each thigh, but they are not nearly as large as in the Spurred. Adults are high-domed and often 12 to 18 inches (30 to 45 cm) long. They are mature at about 12 inches (30 cm) and are not easy to sex, the males being larger than females and with a longer tail and slightly concave posterior plastron (as might be expected).

This tortoise can be kept indoors if you can devote a room to it and

PHOTO BY P. A. RUTLEDGE

Unattended dogs should never be left with a tortoise. Even the friendliest dog may attack and damage a turtle during play.

provide sufficient heat and lighting, but it is better off outdoors, keeping it in a somewhat scaled down version of a Spur house. Its keeping requirements are similar to those of the Spur as well, but it may be getting a bit

PHOTO BY P. A. RUTLEDGE

Young African Spurs need a varied vegetable and fruit diet with plenty of calcium and vitamin supplementation if they are to grow steadily and have the correct carapace shape.

PHOTO BY P. A. RUTLEDGE

Though they commonly are bred today, *Geochelone sulcata* still are expensive tortoises that find a ready market. Thefts of these (and other) tortoises are not unheard of.

more adaptable to higher humidities as more generations are captive-bred. A limited amount of dog food seems to do them no harm, but be careful that babies do not get too much animal protein.

Breeding of this species has become rather common in captivity. Females lay several clutches of 10 to 15 eggs each year (with occasional clutches of 24 to 30 recorded), so it is a prolific species that can make a profit for its breeder in a few years. The eggs hatch in 180 to 240 days on average, depending on the temperature. The babies are among the most beautiful of the turtles, being brightly marked with a blackish brown circle around each scute, a reddish brown circle inside each scute, and a bright reddish brown spot to the back of center in the vertebral and costal scutes. As it grows the reddish brown fades and the blackish brown breaks up into smaller and smaller spots to produce the adult pattern. Expect babies to be mature in about four years.

Leopard Tortoises have gained a reputation as big, friendly, personable pets, and they are among the most popular turtles. Though expensive, a subadult Leopard may be the perfect beginner's tortoise, especially if you have a large backyard and do not live in an exceptionally cool, wet climate.

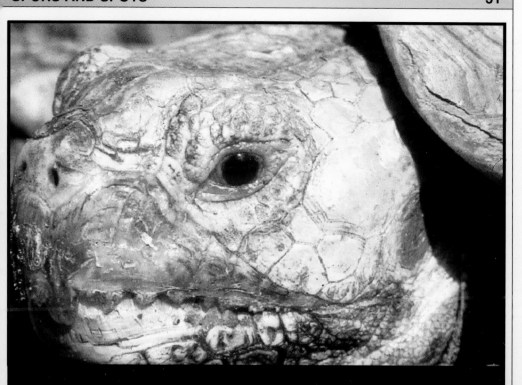

Above: Although tortoises lack teeth, that doesn't mean they can't produce vicious bites. The jaw edges (tomia) of this large African Spur, *Geochelone sulcata*, are deeply notched through wear to produce pseudoteeth. Photo by R.D. Bartlett

Below: Portrait of a "typical" African Spur. Photo by R.D. Bartlett

Mating *Geochelone sulcata*.

A young (notice there is only one growth ring) *Geochelone sulcata* showing the heavy scalation of the front leg.

A stunningly marked Leopard Tortoise, *Geochelone pardalis*. Many young specimens are this beautiful, though old adults may become more brownish with weaker patterns.

PHOTO BY K. H. SWITAK

"Tail view" of a female Leopard Tortoise, *Geochelone pardalis*, showing the rather small conical spurs on the thighs and the short tail.

PHOTO BY J. R. LOLL

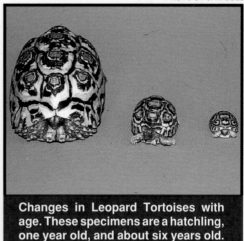

Changes in Leopard Tortoises with age. These specimens are a hatchling, one year old, and about six years old.

PHOTO BY K. H. SWITAK

Courtship before mating in a wild pair of Leopard Tortoises. This photo, taken in Gemsbok Park in the Kalahari, gives a good idea of the natural habitat of the species.

RED, YELLOW, AND BROWN FEET

Among the very best of the pet tortoises are the Red-footed (*Geochelone carbonaria*) and the Yellow-footed (*G. denticulata*) Tortoises (subgenus *Chelonoidis*) from South America. These are fairly large species (usually over a foot, 30 cm, long) that adapt well to humid climates and can tolerate for short periods temperatures well below 60°F (16°C). They also are colorful, an unusual characteristic for larger tortoises, personable, and breed easily in captivity. Their close relative the Chaco Tortoise, in contrast, is a plain brown species that is difficult to maintain in captivity.

PHOTO BY Z. TAKACS

Head view of a well-marked Red-footed Tortoise, *Geochelone carbonaria*. The amount of red on the head varies greatly in this species, as does the color of the spots on the front legs.

RED-FOOTS

Geochelone carbonaria is a striking tortoise. Typical adults are 12 to 18 inches (30 to 45 cm) long, with a black or very dark brown carapace marked with discrete yellow to orange spots on the oldest central part of each scute (the areola). The front legs have heavy, pointed scales, some of which are scarlet in color, and the head is brightly marked with orange or even bright cherry red (especially specimens from Paraguay and Argentina) blotches and stripes. Southern specimen often have the area around the nostrils swollen and bulbous. Red-foots are tortoises of humid forests on the edges of savannahs over much of northern South America (into eastern Panama) south to the eastern Amazon and also in a broad belt from central Brazil to Argentina and Paraguay. There is a broad gap in its range south of the Amazon River where it does not occur. It likes warm, humid surroundings, where it hides in debris on the forest floor. Both it and the Yellow-foot can be found together in much of northern South America.

Husbandry

If at all possible, allow your Red-foot to spend most of the day outdoors during suitable weather. They enjoy grazing on grass and alfalfa and also take chopped fruits and vegetables of all types. Adults can be fed canned dog food and also monkey pellets on a limited basis, though this type of food probably is too rich in protein to feed to juveniles as more than an occasional treat.

These turtles enjoy grazing during warm summer rains, when most of their breeding activity is likely to occur. When the temperature reaches much above 90°F (32°C) they seek shade and water to soak in. They can tolerate cool nights down to about 50°F

tortoises should be moved indoors during the winter and kept warm; they are active all year.

Breeding

Red-foots grow rapidly, reaching sexual maturity and much of their full adult size by four years of age. If fed heavily on animal foods and kept constantly warm, they may mature in under three years, but this is not recommended.

Breeding is much like that in

PHOTO BY R. D. BARTLETT

This Red-footed Tortoise, *Geochelone carbonaria*, actually has red leg scales (the feet are never red, just the leg scales). Some populations of this species have the shell pinched-in at the center, as in this specimen.

(10°C), but anything below this for more than a night or two should be avoided. If given a shed that is free from drafts and has a basking light and water, they soon learn to go to bed in it when the weather gets too cool for their liking. As always, adults are much more tolerant of drafts and coolness than are babies, which are best kept indoors in a large, warm, lighted terrarium for their first year or two. All these

other large tortoises. Males are recognizable by their much longer, flattened tails and, in most populations, the distinctly constricted sides of the shell giving it something of a dumbbell shape. Males check the species and sex of another turtle by swinging their heads and looking for appropriate responses. They then sniff the female's cloaca and go through the usual following, butting, and leg biting routines. Males produce chuckling or clucking noises during mating.

Females lay two or more clutches per year, each with from six to over a dozen rounded to somewhat elongated eggs. The nest hole usually is shallow, just a few inches, and the whole egg-laying sequence may be completed in just a few hours. The eggs should be removed to an incubator (vermiculite and water at about a 1:1 or 1:2 ratio) and maintained between 81 and 86°F (27 and 30°C) for four to six months, occasionally opening the incubator to let things "breathe."

PHOTO BY R. D. BARTLETT

A young (notice the growth rings) "cherry head" Red-footed Tortoise from Paraguay. Such brightly marked specimens are worth a high premium and may be selectively bred.

The babies are about 2 inches (5 cm) long, rounded, and brown and yellow like most similar tortoises. The anterior marginals are smooth-edged. Babies can be put outdoors in protected pens when the temperature rises above 60°F (16°C), but beware of cloudy days and drafts.

YELLOW-FOOTS

The Yellow-footed Tortoise, *Geochelone denticulata*, is very similar to the Red-foot, and the two often are confused. Its carapace is a paler brown than most Red-foots, and there typically is a large, somewhat irregular orangish or yellowish blotch in each scute (smaller, with distinct edge, and usually brighter in the Red-foot). The front legs have yellow to bright orange, not red, scales, and the head usually is patterned in some shade of bright yellow to orange. The sides of the carapace in both sexes are straight to slightly convex, not concave as in many males of the Red-foot.

Though the sizes of the two species overlap greatly, Yellow-foots are on average a bit larger than Red-foots, with records to about 30 inches (75 cm) and 100 pounds (45 kilos). It also is a species of humid tropical forests and is even less likely to be found on dry savannahs than is the Red-foot. It is found over much of northern and central South American east of the Andes but does not go as far south or northwest as the Red-foot, though it tolerates the flood basin forests of the Amazon better.

In virtually all respects the care and breeding of the Yellow-foot is like that for the Red-foot. Both species have about the same feeding needs and react the same to warm rains and cool nights. They are best housed outdoors (especially large specimens) most of the year and learn to go into their warm shed on their own when the evening temperature drops below 50°F (10°C) or so.

Females lay two clutches per year, sometimes more, each with 4 to 12 or more eggs. Incubation is much as in Red-foot. Babies are yellow and brown like little Red-foots, but the corners of the anterior marginals are toothed, distinctly pointed and projecting (the origin of the species name *denticulata*, toothed). The young grow fast once they start eating (many do not feed for a week or two after leaving the egg) and are mature in about four years at 10 to 12 inches (25 to 30 cm) shell length.

Both the Red-foot and the Yellow-foot are excellent pets that feed well, especially half-grown two-year-olds that have been captive-bred. These turtles are used extensively for food in South America and are losing their forests to development, so it is not ecologically sound to purchase wild-caught specimens.

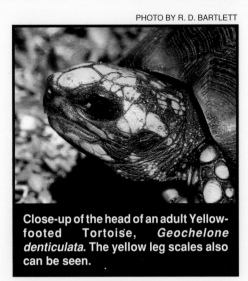

Close-up of the head of an adult Yellow-footed Tortoise, *Geochelone denticulata*. The yellow leg scales also can be seen.

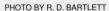

Notice the strong teeth or denticles on the anterior marginals of this hatchling Yellow-footed Tortoise, *Geochelone denticulata*.

THE CHACO TORTOISE

The third South American tortoise (excluding the giants of the Galapagos Islands) is not well-established in the hobby and remains poorly understood. This is *Geochelone chilensis*, which does not occur in Chile but instead is a species of Paraguay and Argentina. At various times it has been heavily collected for the pet trade, but it does not do especially well in captivity and seldom reproduces.

There is a great amount of variation in shape and size in this species, and it has led to the description of two types: *donosobarrosi*—large, oval, more southern; and *petersi*—small, elongate, more northern. Today these are considered to be synonyms of *chilensis*, but some doubt remains as to exactly what is happening in this species. Regardless, the Chaco Tortoise is moderate in size, 8 to 16 inches (20 to 40 cm) long, with a sandy brown carapace that usually is unmarked or has dark brown staining on the

PHOTO BY K. H. SWITAK

"Tail view" of a Choco Tortoise, *Geochelone chilensis*, showing the group of conical scales on the backs of the thighs. The very short tail may indicate a female, but this species is hard to sex.

pronounced growth rings. The head and legs are brown, the front legs unmarked but with some extremely heavy scales, and there are enlarged tubercles at the back of the thigh. It is an inhabitant of dry, shrubby savannah and desert where rains are infrequent, the summers are extremely hot, and the winters may be quite cold. Specimens from the northern part of the range winter in shallow depressions (called pallets in tortoises), while those from the southern part of the range dig actual burrows to get away from the cold, much like the gopher tortoises.

Sexes are difficult to distinguish. In this species the males typically are somewhat smaller than females and lighter in build with only slightly longer tails. Males may have broader heads than females from the same population and usually are more brightly colored, but the enlarged scales on their front legs tend to be dark brown rather than yellowish tan as in females. In nature, females lay a clutch of two (sometimes six) eggs

in February or March (the southern summer). Hatching apparently takes a full year in nature, but as little as four months in captivity. The young are rather flattened, circular, and almost uniformly brown. They grow slowly because they must spend most of the winter months inactive, and it is possible they may not be sexually mature until at least 12 years old. Dry grasses, cacti, and other plants provide most of the food in nature, but in captivity they take the usual veggie salad and drink liberally. Unlike the Red-footed and Yellow-footed Tortoises, Chaco Tortoises should be brumated during the winter months.

In many ways the Chaco Tortoise has evolved in parallel to the North American gopher tortoises, and they may be confused with them. *Gopherus* species have a cervical scute, however, that is absent in *Geochelone chilensis*. They present many of the same difficulties in captive care as gopher tortoises and similarly are being reduced in number by excessive collecting and loss of their marginal habitat. Until captive-bred Chaco Tortoises become more common, it is best that beginners pass this species by.

Young Choco Tortoises are very slow-growing.

ASIAN STARS AND BROWNS

THE STARS

This chapter covers a variety of Asian (and Madagascan) *Geochelone* species that are allied more by color patterns than by real structural characters. The four species of starred tortoises of the genus *Geochelone* (there are other starred tortoises in other genera) form two species pairs. One pair is the Asian stars, consisting of the Indian Star Tortoise, *G. elegans*, from India and Sri Lanka, and the rare and poorly known Burmese Star Tortoise *G. platynota*, from southern Burma. The other pair is the Madagascan radiated tortoises, consisting of the Radiated Tortoise, *G. radiata*, from southern Madagascar, and the Angulated Tortoise, *G. yniphora*, from northwestern Madagascar. In both cases one species of the pair is fairly easy to obtain and the other is rare as rare can be.

THE INDIAN STAR TORTOISE

One of the most beautiful tortoises, both in color and in form, is *Geochelone elegans*, a common species that occurs over most of India and Sri Lanka in all types of habitats, from seasonally wet monsoon forests to near-desert. At a maximum size of about 11 inches (28 cm), it is not too large for many apartments and thus is popular in the northeastern United States where outdoor arrangements for tortoises may be difficult to achieve. The carapace is very highly domed, and each vertebral and costal scute is individually produced into a low pyramid, accentuating the bright yellow centers and narrow radiating yellow lines of the color pattern. The background color of the carapace is deep brownish black, in high contrast with the yellow stars. The plastron is yellow with black radiating lines, and the head and legs are mostly pale yellowish brown. A more beautiful animal can hardly be imagined.

Unfortunately, this is not always an easy species to maintain. For unknown reasons it seems to be sensitive to long periods of high humidity. Try to maintain it with a mixture of outdoor grazing on warm, dry

PHOTO BY K. H. SWITAK

A typical, well-marked Indian Star Tortoise, *Geochelone elegans*.

days and a heated, lighted, large terrarium on cooler or more humid days. Captive-bred pets may be more adaptable than wild-caught ones, but admittedly at the moment all specimens are somewhat chancey. They feed well on veggie salad and fruits plus the usual treats of dog or cat food occasionally (not too much, please). Try to keep the terrarium

PHOTO BY R. D. BARTLETT

As the Indian Star grows, the scutes become blacker and the yellow is restricted to radiating lines.

PHOTO BY R. D. BARTLETT

A very young captive-bred Indian Star Tortoise, *Geochelone elegans*, displaying the distinctive pattern.

temperature at about 80 to 86°F (27 to 30°C) with a mixture of basking lights and undertank heating. Make sure water is always available.

Females lay relatively few (usually five to seven) eggs in a clutch but produce many clutches (as many as eight or nine) in a year. The hatchlings are black and yellow-orange but lack the radiating yellow stars of the adults.

For many years the Indian Star was one of the most common pet tortoises, but in the 1970's exports from India virtually

ceased and there were not enough breeding animals in captivity to maintain the species as a regularly available pet. Recently exports have begun again and wild-caught adults are available at rather low prices. Be sure to have your new pet vetted as soon as you get it and be sure to quarantine it. As captive-breds become more available because the species is being bred regularly, a higher quality pet should result.

PHOTO BY R. D. BARTLETT

A nicely marked Indian Star, *Geochelone elegans*. These beautiful animals may be difficult to establish if you have a wild-caught adult.

PHOTO BY R. D. BARTLETT

A very young Radiated Tortoise, *Geochelone radiata*. The pattern of the shell is much like that of a young Indian Star.

The Rare Burmese Star

The related Burmese Star (*G. platynota*) seldom is seen in the hobby and currently is unavailable to the average hobbyist. It closely resembles the Indian but has a less complicated star pattern on the carapace with fewer radiating yellow lines; the plastron is yellow with black triangular blotches rather than yellow with radiating yellow lines

as in the Indian. Few animals presently are being exported from Burma because of political problems, but that could change at any time. Unfortunately, the Burmese Star is reported to be a favorite stewpot turtle, and it is quite possible that populations are being overcollected.

PHOTO BY P. FREED

Indian Stars, *Geochelone elegans*, usually have yellow and black (mostly yellow) heads and lack a cervical scute over the neck.

THE RADIATED TORTOISE

Madagascar is the home of two large, highly domed tortoises. Both are listed as endangered (Appendix I on the CITES list), but the Radiated Tortoise (*Geochelone radiata*) is available as captive-bred specimens if you have a large budget and are willing to go through the red tape necessary to legally possess one. This is a 16-inch (40-cm) tortoise that appears massive because of the extremely high doming of the shell. The dark brown to blackish carapace has a bright yellow starred pattern similar to that of the Indian Star but a bit more simple. The legs and head are bright yellow,

PHOTO BY R. D. BARTLETT

Radiated Tortoises, *Geochelone radiata*, usually have mostly black heads and a distinct cervical scute over the neck.

though the top of the head often has a black blotch near the center. The plastron is bright yellow with large triangular black blotches and sometimes a trace of radiating yellow lines. Both this species and the similar Angulated Tortoise have shells that appear to be evenly rounded because the centers of the vertebrals and costals are not individually domed as in the Indian Star.

This species is from dry scrublands of southern Madagascar, where it feeds on grasses, fruits, and succulent plants. It is easy to maintain if the humidity is kept relatively low. They do well outdoors most of the year and can be moved into a heated tortoise shed on wet days and during the winter. Males may not mature until they are over 12 inches (30 cm) long.

Radiated Tortoises have been bred in captivity since at least 1973, and today several zoos and private breeders produce a good number of animals each year. Females produce as many as six clutches of eggs each year, each with about six eggs, so they are quite prolific. Incubation can be very prolonged if the temperature is kept low (five to ten or even 12 months), but at incubator temperatures near 86°F (30°C) the eggs may hatch in as few as three months. Unlike the Indian Star, babies are marked much like adults, but the radiating stars are white rather than yellow.

Rarest of the Rare

The exceedingly rare (probably fewer than 400 animals left in the wilds of northwestern Madagascar) Angulated Tortoise or Angonoka (*G. yniphora*) is much like the Radiated Tortoise but lacks the starred pattern on the bright brown carapace and has an almost unmarked plastron. The anterior scute of the plastron (gular scute) is single, very long, and curves upward in this species, while in the Radiated Tortoise the gular scutes are paired, not very long, and not strongly up-curved. Though captive-bred both in Madagascar and in several zoos, private ownership is very difficult because of the endangered status of the species. In Madagascar it is a popular food animal (as is the Radiated Tortoise) and its habitat in dry bamboo forests rapidly is being destroyed. It is unlikely that either species has much future in their native homes.

THE BROWNS

The Mountain Tortoise, *Manouria emys*, is a primitive relative of the genus *Geochelone* and often is included in that genus. Its other common name, Asian Brown Tortoise, is quite descriptive because the species is uniformly dark brown to olive brown over the carapace and has blackish legs and a dark head. The plastron is yellowish with strong brown shading. Though widely distributed in highland forests from northern India and Bangladesh through Burma and Thailand to Sumatra and Borneo, this species only recently has become available in the hobby in reasonable numbers. At the

PHOTO BY B. CHRISTIE

The very rare Angulated Tortoise, *Geochelone yniphora*, is a big brown tortoise recognized by the single long, often curved gular scute below the neck.

moment only the northern subspecies, *M. e. phayrei*, found from northern India to central Thailand is seen. This type has a distinctly domed carapace up to 24 inches (60 cm) long and at first glance looks much like a Gopher Tortoise, *Gopherus polyphemus*. However, it is easily distinguished by the group of large spurs or tubercles at the back of the thigh; these may be so large that they look like an extra pair of legs, thus the alternative common name Six-legged Tortoise.

This species likes it wet and perfers moderate temperatures. In nature it has been seen foraging for aquatic plants and bulbs in forest streams, a very unusual behavior for a tortoise. In captivity it likes to graze outdoors, especially during warm, showery days, and enjoys lawn sprinklers. Try to maintain it at temperatures between 60 and 80°F (16 and 27°C) and humidities over 70%. Like Red-foots, it does not like day after day of hot, dry weather.

Females lay numerous eggs (as many as 50!) in a gigantic mound of damp leaf litter built by the female on the forest floor. She is reported to actually guard the eggs for a few days after laying. Two clutches may be laid each year. Very little has been reported about the captive-breeding of this species, which has occurred mostly in zoos but recently has been successful with private breeders as well. The young are about 2 inches (5 cm) long like most other tortoises and are brown with paler brown centers to the scutes. They have an odd wrinkled appearance due to strong growth rings around the areolae of the scutes. Fairly delicate, they should not be put outdoors until at least nine months old. They and their parents are most active at dusk and dawn (they are not fond of basking in the sun) and feed best when sprinkled or the weather is showery. The young desiccate rapidly if the humidity drops below 70%, and you may have to install an automatic misting system in their terrarium. They feed on a variety of greens and vegetables as well as fruits. At least one breeder has stated that dog food and monkey biscuits may cause severe deformities in the young and should never be fed.

The southern subspecies, *M. e. emys*, is a smaller tortoise not much over 18 inches (45 cm) with a distinctly flattened carapace. It is reported to lay much smaller egg clutches, only five to eight eggs at a time. In some respects it is more similar to the other species of *Manouria*, the rare and very poorly known Impressed Tortoise (*M. impressa*) from Southeast Asia. That species, which is virtually unknown in captivity and apparently is declining in nature, is a pale yellowish brown with distinctly

PHOTO BY R. D. BARTLETT

An attractively marked Elongated Tortoise, *Geochelone elongata*. The pale head is said to become pinkish during the breeding season, but this is not always observed in captivity.

PHOTO BY J. R. LOLL

A breeding pair of Elongated Tortoises, *Geochelone elongata*.

produced, serrated posterior marginals. The babies are reported to be heavily keeled and serrated much like one of the spiny turtles of the genus *Heosemys*. Perhaps someday they will appear in the hobby.

ELONGATED TORTOISES

Just a few words are necessary about the foot-long (30-cm) Elongated Tortoise, *Geochelone (Indotestudo) elongata*. This species of southern Asia in much like the Mountain Tortoise in habitat requirements and feeding needs (though it likes a bit of animal protein every now and then), but it is reported to be a very aggressive, actually mean, tortoise that may have to be kept individually (like *Testudo* species). The clutches are small, only two or three eggs at a time, and the species is not bred in large numbers. The carapace is narrow, not very high-domed, and usually is a dull brown color with darker brown and blackish blotches and specks. The head usually is very pale, almost whitish, and is reported to become bright pink during breeding. Perhaps if it were to become more common as captive-bred specimens it would be appealing to specialists just because of its odd head color.

Though it has its admirers, the Mountain, Burmese, or Brown Tortoise, *Manouria emys*, never will be called a colorful species. This plain brown tortoise has proved hard to breed in captivity but finally is being produced in small numbers. *Manouria* is one of many generic names that may be treated as subgenera of *Geochelone*. Above: R. D. Bartlett; Below: A. Norman

THE ULTIMATE GIANTS

Though they don't really belong in a beginner's book on tortoises, we can't get by without a few words on the true giant tortoises, the Galapagos Giant Tortoise (*Geochelone nigra*, formerly *G. elephantopus*) and the Aldabra Giant Tortoise (*G. gigantea*).

ALDABRAS

The Aldabra Giant Tortoise is the last remnant of what once were perhaps dozens of species of gigantic tortoises that evolved on islands in the Indian Ocean. Similarly gigantic species also evolved in North America and the Asiatic mainland, but they became extinct long before civilized man reached these areas. On islands the tortoises lasted much longer, and many were still alive when Europeans and Asians settled the Indian Ocean. Of course, large tortoises make excellent food, and they soon were devoured to extinction. Aldabras managed to survive in isolation and today are numerous on the sparsely settled islands north of Madagascar as well as in parks around the world.

PHOTO BY K. H. SWITAK

Head-on view of a captive-hatched Galapagos Giant Tortoise, *Geochelone nigra*, about three years old. Notice the round nostrils located well above the mouth.

Geochelone gigantea deserves its scientific name because the Aldabra is the largest living tortoise, measuring in at a carapace length of 56 inches (140 cm) and a weight of at least 560 pounds (255 kilos); it is at least 8 inches (20 cm) longer than the longest Galapagos Giant and heavier as well. (Some authorities believe that these figures are greatly exaggerated, and they may be right.) Of course tortoises this size are not keepable in average backyards, but they often are seen in zoos and parks. They have a rather low, broad, blackish carapace that usually has a distinct cervical scute. Captive specimens often have greatly distorted scutes because of improper diets.

Females lay eggs several times a year in nature if the population size is small, but they lay only every few years if the population numbers are high. They are true omnivores, feeding on almost any type of vegetation from grasses to fruits and vegetables and also like animal protein, being reported to actually crush small pigs and chickens beneath their plastra and then eat them. Captive-bred specimens occasionally are available.

GALAPAGOS GIANTS

One of the most complex taxonomic problems in the turtles concerns just how many species or subspecies of Galapagos Giant Tortoise exist. The name of the species recently was changed from the very familiar *Geochelone elephantopus* (singularly appropriate for this elephant-footed species) to the strange *G. nigra*, a change that not all specialists accept. At least 12 names currently are applied to various island forms, but since the tortoises have been moved about so much from island to island in attempts to maintain or reestablish populations, have on occasion been interbred, and are extremely variable anyway, recognition of these subspecies or species is merely an academic exercise. Suffice it to say that the species reaches about 48 inches in length (120 cm) and 500 pounds (225 kilos) in weight and varies in carapace shape from very flattened to extremely domed.

PHOTO BY R. D. BARTLETT

A captive-bred hatchling Aldabra Giant Tortoise, *Geochelone gigantea*. Notice the pointed snout.

Some forms, the so-called saddlebacks, have the front of the shell extremely elevated in males, apparently an adaptation related to fights between males (the one with the longer neck and higher saddle can extend above an opponent with less development) and perhaps to selective foraging on tree-like cacti. Not all Galapagos Giants are very big, by the way.

The Galapagos Giant Tortoise is the main tourist attraction of the virtually barren Galapagos Island group west of Ecuador. Tourist ships stop at regular schedules, debark the tourists for tours of pens with various sizes of tortoises, everyone pays their landing and park usage fees, and everyone is happy. Unfortunately, increasing numbers of pirate fishermen and illegal settlers have developed a taste for tortoise flesh, and once again the tortoises are facing doom.

Captive-bred Galapagos Giants are readily available to keepers with the proper facilities and permits. They breed fairly well in warm, dry areas such as California and Arizona, and once established they are hardy and very long-lived. Like the Aldabras

Above: A mating pair of *Geochelone nigra hoodensis* near Darwin Station on Santa Cruz, the Galapagos. This is one of the "saddlebacked" subspecies. Photo: K. H. Switak. Below: A mating pair (plus a single) of the Aldabra Giant Tortoise, *Geochelone gigantea*, in a park. The scientific names of the two giant tortoises have changed several times recently and the two species often are confused in zoos and parks. Photo: U. E. Friese.

PHOTO BY R. D. BARTLETT

A young Galapagos Giant Tortoise, *Geochelone nigra*, showing the typical flat face. This species is more commonly known as *G. elephantopus*, now considered a synonym.

Giant, this species is known to live over 100 years and is reputed to perhaps reach the two century mark.

ALDABRA GIANTS VERSUS GALAPAGOS GIANTS

The giant tortoises often are confused even by park keepers, and it is not unusual to see mixed groups of the two species under one label. Big, dark brown or blackish tortoises, often with greatly deformed shells, look much alike at first glance. Galapagos Giants usually lack the cervical scute, but not all Aldabras have this scute. However, a glance at the face should be sufficient to tell the two apart. In the Aldabra Giant the head is distinctly wedge-shaped with vertical, slit-like nostrils at the end of a projecting, somewhat pointed snout. The nostrils are not far above the mouth. The Galapagos Giant, on the other hand, has a flattened, rather pugged face with rounded nostrils located well above the mouth. From the side the face appears to have a vertical silhouette. This difference works much better than looking at the carapace.

AFRICAN BEAUTIES

Africa is home to many tortoises, more than any other continent, and many are small and brightly colored species that long have been of interest to hobbyists. In this chapter we'll briefly talk about five genera, few of which are easily available in the pet hobby. All have their advocates, however, and occasionally captive-bred specimens of a few can be found if you have the patience and the money. However, in many cases you would be better off saving your money and taking a trip to parks and reserves in southern and western Africa to see the tortoises in their natural habitat. South Africa protects several species in preserves and restricts their export.

PHOTO BY K. H. SWITAK

A hatchling Bowsprit Tortoise, *Chersina angulata*, from South Africa.

THE BOWSPRIT TORTOISE

Chersina angulata, often called the Angulate Tortoise in the African literature, long has been known as the Bowsprit Tortoise because of the long, single, projecting gular scale at the anterior end of the plastron similar to the projecting bow on a sailing ship. This beautiful tortoise reaches 12 inches (30 cm) in length, but usually is much smaller, and has an elongated, highly domed carapace that is pinched in at the center in some males. The carapace has a distinctive long slope at the front with a deep notch at the center. It is dark brown, glossy, with a yellow ring on each costal and vertebral and wide yellow triangles on the marginals. The head and legs are dark brown.

Bowsprits inhabit sandy, scrubby, near-deserts in southwestern Africa, where they feed on dry grasses, succulents, and whatever other vegetation they can find. In captivity they are delicate and cannot stand high humidity. They feed on assorted vegetables (especially legumes) and even the common garden portulaca, a semi-succulent plant. They occasionally have been bred in captivity, laying one or two eggs per clutch several times a year. The eggs hatch in about three to eight months. Sexual maturity may take 12 years, so removing

PHOTO BY K. H. SWITAK

Dorsal view of a Bowsprit Tortoise, *Chersina angulata*, from Addo Elephant Park, South Africa.

currently five species are recognized, though there are several subspecies and supposed synonyms that probably will some day be raised to species level. They are the smallest tortoises, seldom exceeding 6 inches (15 cm) and occasionally not making it to 4 inches (10 cm) in adults. The shell is flat or very low, with the scutes not raised in pyramids like *Psammobates*. Most are brownish with weakly developed patterns of dull yellow rings on dark brown or blackish spots on brown. Males have nearly flat plastrons and long tails.

Cape tortoises have proved virtually impossible to keep for very long in captivity outside South Africa. They are dwellers in very dry, rocky plains and deserts, where they frequent

any specimens from natural populations means doom to the tortoises.

Once these tortoises were imported in tremendous numbers and were available cheaply in pet shops. However, almost all died within a few months, being unable to stand the moist conditions in the United States and Europe. They are as hard or harder to keep than gopher tortoises and cannot be recommended even for experts. Fortunately their export from South Africa now is prohibited. A very few captive-bred specimens find their way to the market occasionally and *might* be worth the investment and paperwork.

CAPE TORTOISES

The genus *Homopus* is found only in South Africa, where

PHOTO BY K. H. SWITAK

Ventral view of a Bowsprit Tortoise. Notice the exceptionally long, single gular scute typical of this species.

scrub and thorn thickets. Females lay only one or two (rarely five) eggs that hatch after four to ten months into babies only an inch or so (2.5 to 3 cm) long. Males can be quite aggressive, and these tortoises might best be kept

brownish background. This species is considerably more domed than the Speckled, which is quite flat, speckled dark brown or black on brown, and has serrated marginals. The Speckled Cape Tortoise is the smallest

A male Speckled Cape Tortoise, *Homopus signatus signatus*, from Springbok, Cape Province, South Africa.

individually. Kept dry and warm, they are long-lived and very slow to mature.

Only the Parrot-beaked Cape Tortoise (*H. areolatus*) is seen on occasion, though the Speckled Cape Tortoise (*H. signatus*) once also was exported from South Africa. The Parrot-beak is interesting because the nose of the male turns a bright rosy orange during breeding season and the entire shell may take on a temporary rosy flush. The centers (areolae) of the scutes are depressed and yellowish on a

tortoise species, not quite reaching 4 inches (10 cm) in shell length.

If you live in a humid climate, don't even think of keeping these tortoises. Perhaps if you could establish a warm, rocky terrarium that has a controlled, dehumidified air source you might have some luck, but it probably would be better to just move to Arizona.

GEOMETRIC TORTOISES

The species of *Psammobates* are delicate little starred tortoises with high-domed carapaces and each scute individually elevated into a low pyramid, much like tiny Indian Star Tortoises (the young of which do not have a starred pattern). They are among the most beautiful of tortoises, but like the other southern African pattern, but has hugely developed corners on the marginals, resulting in one of the most distinctive outlines among the tortoises.

The Tent Tortoise, *Psammobates tentorius*, has been imported in the past but currently

The rosy orange snout of this Parrot-beaked Cape Tortoise, *Homopus areolatus*, gives it a lot of character. Some specimens (especially males) have much more color on the shell, but even dull specimens are more colorful than most tortoises. Unfortunately, this species is virtually unavailable.

dwellers in dry, sandy, or rocky plains and deserts, they are very delicate and never do well in captivity. In most respects they are much like *Homopus*, being long-lived (well over 20 years) and laying few eggs. They cannot tolerate high humidity and seldom live in captivity. Few specimens exceed 6 inches (15 cm) in shell length. One species, the Serrated Star Tortoise, *P. oculiferus*, not only has a beautifully starred is protected and seldom seen. At almost 6 inches (15 cm) it is a giant in the genus, but most specimens are almost 2 inches shorter. Females lay one or two eggs that hatch in about nine months. This is an amazingly variable tortoise that has been named at least 20 times and may actually represent a gigantic complex of similar species or subspecies. Males are much smaller than females and have an almost flat plastron.

THE PANCAKE TORTOISE

The most unusual tortoise is the Pancake. There can be no exception to this statement because, quite simply, it is true. Pancakes have adapted to dry, never stray far from cover, they exist as many isolated populations that vary in color and size to some extent. Most are about 5 inches (12.5 cm) long and brownish with a vaguely radiating yellowish pattern. They feed well on the usual veggie salad and

A Serrated or Kalahari Star Tortoise, *Psammobates oculiferus*, looks like an Indian Star at first glance but has projecting edges (serrae) on the marginal scutes. Babies are especially saw-edged.

rocky regions of Tanzania and Kenya, where they escape predators by running under boulders and wedging themselves in with their strong claws. To do this successfully they have sacrificed the rigidity of a typical tortoise's shell, becoming greatly flattened with a flexible shell that is as much open space as bone under the horny scutes. They are fast runners and excellent climbers, making the best of their attempted return to the non-shelled ancestors of the turtles.

Because Pancakes are restricted to rocky areas and related foods, taking only a bit of animal protein occasionally. Males are not especially aggressive except when mating. They are smaller and brighter than females and have the usual longer tail. Only one egg is laid at a time, but a female may lay several times a year. The egg is distinctly elongated, as contrasted to the round eggs of most other tortoises.

Pancakes are not that hard to keep, and they have been imported for over a decade in large numbers. There are several captive-breeding programs in effect for these tortoises, but almost all the specimens you are likely to see for sale are wild-caught specimens exported from Tanzania. Recent observations from Tanzania indicate that too many specimens are being collected for the species to maintain its populations successfully, and it has been recommended that exports be restricted or stopped completely. However, Tanzania needs money and it is likely that it will take a lots of political haggling to completely stop exports. More concerted efforts at captive-breeding definitely are necessary if these strange tortoises are to remain in the hobby.

PHOTO BY K. H. SWITAK

This exceptionally well-marked Pancake Tortoise, *Malacochersus tornieri*, has an almost jewel-like quality to the scute patterns.

PHOTO BY K. H. SWITAK

This young Pancake Tortoise, *Malacochersus tornieri*, gives an idea of just how flat this species really is. Adults in zoo displays often wedge themselves sideways or upside-down between large rocks and are perfectly comfortable.

HINGE-BACKS

Many different turtles have developed hinges on the plastron to aid in closing the shell off from predators. In the genus *Kinixys*, however, a hinge is developed across the back of the *carapace*, allowing the posterior part of the shell to close off the hind legs. Hatchlings are flattened and have serrated marginals, and they lack the hinge, looking much like Cape tortoises (*Homopus*) or tiny *Heosemys* spiny turtles. Fortunately for identification purposes all *Kinixys* occur north of the range of Cape tortoise species, and most of them are inhabitants of moist tropical forests or the forest-savannah edge. Western African countries currently are exporting fair numbers of at least two species, so hinge-backs are seen with some regularity in the hobby. Unfortunately, they seldom do well in captivity.

Except for *K. natalensis*, a poorly understood form from dry plains in South Africa, the hinge-backs like it warm and humid. Provide temperatures in the middle or upper 80's F (about 30°C), a humidity over 70%, and a large water area for bathing and (!) swimming (yes, these tortoises swim moderately well). If you keep them outdoors, be sure the

Pyxis planicauda, the Flat-shelled Tortoise, is a rare Madagascar species often placed in the genus *Acinixys*.

Kinixys erosa, the Forest Hinge-back Tortoise, has strongly developed corners on the posterior marginal scutes.

Bell's Hinge-back, *Kinixys belliana*, is quite variable. The specimen shown here belongs to the subspecies (or full species) *K. b. speki* of southeastern Africa.

temperature does not drop below about 70°F (21°C) for more than a few hours. The legs of these tortoises are relatively slender and long, and the tortoises move with an unusual gait. They often feed on animal protein as well as the usual vegetables, digging snails and millipedes out of the forest litter and even fishing for snails, shrimp, and fishes in shallow water at the edges of streams.

The carapace of hinge-backs is elongated and usually brown with subdued yellow patterns of circles and/or radiating lines. In *Kinixys erosa* of western and central Africa the posterior marginals are strongly serrated. In the West African *K. homeana* the back of the shell in adults descends at almost a right angle to the rest of the carapace, resulting in the very appropriate German common name of Clipped Tortoise—the animal actually looks like the back of the shell has been cut off. The widely distributed *K. belliana* occurs from Senegal to Somalia and south to Natal, living in rather dry forests at the edges of savannahs, but it also enjoys humid quarters when it can get them. This is an especially variable tortoise with many described subspecies (including one with only four claws on the front feet) and many localized variants.

Breeding of the hinge-backs in captivity is rare. *K. belliana* lays two to seven elongate eggs that hatch in about three to four months in natural surroundings. Females may lay every six weeks or so. One successful breeding of

K. homeana in Germany yielded three young that hatched 119 to 127 days after laying when kept at temperatures between 81 and 90°F (27 and 32°C). In a bit over a year the young grew from under 2 inches (4 cm) to 5 inches (13 cm) on a diet of earthworms, fish, and raw meat. The flattened juvenile shell did not begin to deepen until the young were a year old. When first hatched they would take only food that was moving, and they did not take any fruit until a year old. This species is quite aggressive when mixed with other turtles, both as adults and young, though they get along fairly well with each other.

Like so many other tortoises, the West African (and probably central African as well) home of these tortoises is threatened by vast deforestation and pollution. Removing specimens from natural habitats just to have them die in captivity certainly is no solution, and hobbyists must develop a way of successfully captive-breeding hinge-backs if they are to remain in the hobby.

MADAGASCAN SPIDERS

Though not strictly African, the two Madagascan species of *Pyxis* deserve a brief mention. Both are small turtles (under 6 inches, 15 cm) with rather flat carapaces that are brown with yellow patterns. In the Spider Tortoise, *P. arachnoides*, of the southwestern Madagascan coast, the shell is covered with a pattern of radiating yellow lines much like that of the starred tortoises. This species is unique among tortoises in having

PHOTO BY R. S. SIMMONS

Bell's Hinge-back Tortoise, *Kinixys belliana*, is one of the most commonly seen hinge-backs and has been bred in captivity on rare occasions.

PHOTO BY J. VISSER

The odd little Natal Hinge-back, *Kinixys natalensis*, differs from the other hinge-backs in several structural characters and also in its ecology, preferring dry plains.

PHOTO BY R. D. BARTLETT

The Madagascan Spider Tortoise, *Pyxis arachnoides*, seldom is available to hobbyists, and its keeping conditions are poorly understood.

PHOTO BY K. H. SWITAK

The seldom-seen African Tent Tortoise, *Psammobates tentorius* (here the subspecies *trimeni*), is one of the smallest tortoises. They seldom survive well outside of southern Africa.

the centers of the scutes are bright reddish brown, making them beautiful little tortoises. The marginals are strongly turned down over the tail and hind legs, much as in Red-footed and Yellow-footed Tortoises; no hinge is developed. It inhabits dry deciduous forest, spending the dry season hidden in the leaf litter and becoming active during the rainy season.

Madagascar is rapidly losing its forests and with them most of the reptiles. Almost any Madagascan animal may be exported on occasion, and a few *Pyxis* specimens are occasionally mentioned in the hobby literature. Both species are protected to some extent and require permits for possession.

a hinge across the front of the plastron that allows the animal to almost close the shell anteriorly. However, not all subspecies (three are recognized) have a movable hinge. A single large egg is laid, but there is almost no information on this species in captivity. This is a species of dry dunes and thorny brush. It feeds on fruits and insect larvae (picked from cow dung).

Pyxis planicauda, the Flat-shelled Tortoise, is known only from a very small area on the western central coast of Madagascar. The distinctly flattened carapace is brown with yellow centers on the vertebrals and costals and a few radiating yellow lines. In some specimens

PHOTO BY J. VISSER

A hatchling Tent Tortoise, *Psammobates tentorius* (here an intergrade between *P. t. tentorius* and *P. t. verroxi*) looks like a blade for a circular saw.

THE UNTOUCHABLES

OK, I'll put it plain and simple: just forget about keeping gopher tortoises, genus *Gopherus*. The four species of this genus occur only in northern Mexico and the southern United States and all are, to at least some extent, protected. Currently a great deal of money is being expended to protect the Desert Tortoise, *G. agassizi*, in California and Nevada, where housing booms are depriving the tortoises of their rather bleak habitat in dry, stony, deserts and plains. Gopher Tortoises, *G. polyphemus*, from Florida and the southeastern United States, currently are given at least token protection in most areas, though they still lose their rolling, sandy habitat to development and are killed by gasoline poured into their burrows in misguided attempts to kill or collect rattlesnakes. In Texas, *G. berlandieri*, the Texas Tortoise is protected though many die on highways and at the hands of tourists who just cannot resist picking up a specimen that wanders through their campground or the parking lot. In Mexico, specimens are picked up and illegally taken north across the border to enter the underground pet trade in protected animals.

PHOTO BY J. R. LOLL

A hatchling and eggs of the Gopher Tortoise, *Gopherus polyphemus*.

Regardless of politics and laws, there is a more compelling reason not to collect or purchase any gopher tortoise: unless you live in the area from which the specimen was taken, it probably will not survive for long. Gopher tortoises all are very specialized animals that do not adapt to captivity. There have been some exceptions to this, of course, but the number of gophers dying in captivity greatly exceeds the number ever bred in captivity.

Until about a million years ago (or considerably less in some areas), North America was home to a variety of tortoises belonging to both *Gopherus* and *Geochelone*. Some of the *Geochelone* were giant species, and they ranged north almost to the Canadian border, living in the warm, very stable prairies and forests that covered much of the central and southern United States. The continual cycle of glaciation and pluvial periods (the first very dry because most water is trapped in icecaps, the latter wet because the icecaps are melting) during the Pleistocene eventually gave way to the present long period of cool winters over much of the United States and even northern Mexico. The northern *Geochelone* species appear to have been unable to adapt to cold nights and possibly never learned to burrow, becoming extinct on the North American continent. *Gopherus* ancestors, however, were adapted to burrowing and survived, though only in specific areas where soil types allowed easy burrow construction and the days were warm enough to allow activity much of the year. Today the gophers are once again at the verge of extinction, and this time they may not be able to adapt to condominiums, automobiles, and gasoline.

THE GOPHERS

The four species of *Gopherus* align themselves into two pairs. One pair consists of the Gopher Tortoise, *G. polyphemus*, of the Southeast and the Bolson Tortoise, *G. flavomarginatus*, of northern Mexico. The latter

PHOTO BY DR. P. C. H. PRITCHARD

The Bolson Tortoise, *Gopherus flavomarginatus*, was an unexpected discovery in northern Mexico.

PHOTO BY R. T. ZAPPALORTI

A large, dark specimen of the Gopher Tortoise, *Gopherus polyphemus*, from Georgia.

species is up to 14 inches (35 cm) long and has a rather low, rounded carapace that is mostly dark brown. Very similar to the Gopher Tortoise in appearance, it was recognized as a distinct species only in 1959, though a few specimens had been collected in the previous century and though to be mislocalized Gophers. Today it is threatened by conversion of its relict prairie habitat into cattle pasture and conversion of specimens into stewpot fillers. The Gopher Tortoise is found from coastal South Carolina to eastern Louisiana, living in sandy pinelands in complicated, deep burrows that it shares with a multitude of other animals, many found only in the burrows. When a Gopher Tortoise population becomes extinct, it takes with it literally dozens of other species of beetles, crickets, flies, and even frogs. It reaches about 10 inches (25 cm) in length and is a wide, heavy tortoise that still is eaten by locals even when protected by law.

The Texas Tortoise, *G. berlandieri*, is found from south-central Texas into northeastern Mexico. At just 8 inches (20 cm) or so in shell length it is the smallest species of the genus, but it also is a bulky species. The brown shell is heavily sculpted with growth lines and the species is quite attractive. It is found in scrubby woodlands and deserts, often near populated areas. Though it can move fairly fast for a tortoise, it is no match for an automobile or a child. Because winters in its range are not severe, it does not dig a true burrow but instead just clears a shallow depression or pallet to which it returns at night after a day's feeding on cactus, grasses, and the occasional insect and snail. It is closely related to the Desert

PHOTO BY K. H. SWITAK

Fighting males of the Desert Tortoise, *Gopherus agassizi*. Notice the heavy, prong-like gular scutes.

PHOTO BY R. D. BARTLETT

The Texas Tortoise, *Gopherus berlandieri*, may be the most attractively patterned gopher tortoise. It still is common in southern Texas.

PHOTO BY K. H. SWITAK

A double handful of hatchling Texas Tortoises, *Gopherus berlandieri*.

Tortoise, *G. agassizi*, found from southwestern Arizona to Utah and California and northwestern Mexico. The deserts in this area often are quite cold at night, and in such situations the tortoises may dig burrows over 25 feet (8 meters) deep in the rocky soil. They feed on the usual variety of grasses, fruits, and small invertebrates.

OBSERVE, DON'T TAKE

If you want to see the gopher tortoises, take a vacation into their home territories and look at them in the wild while you still can. The Texas, Desert, and Gopher Tortoises are still common in some areas and can be easy to find with a bit of local guidance. When warmed up and hunting in the shade at the edge of the sun (direct sun will kill most tortoises, and gophers are not exceptions), they will give you a merry chase for a few yards while you try to focus a camera on them. If you must move a gopher, be sure to put it back exactly where you found it, because these animals have very strongly defined home ranges and territories, often producing distinctive turtle trails from the burrows to favorite feeding areas. Gopher Tortoises even may lay their eggs at the edges of their burrows in the flattened "porch" of compacted soil. I'm not aware of tours to see the Bolson Tortoise, but perhaps they eventually will be offered, hopefully before the animal becomes extinct except for a few specimens in a zoo somewhere.